CW00515883

Guingamor, Lanval, Tyolet, The Were-Wolf:

Four lais rendered into English prose

Marie De France

The present edition is a reproduction of 1910 publication of this work. Minor typographical errors may have been corrected without note, however, for an authentic reading experience the spelling, punctuation, and capitalization have been retained from the original text.

Preface

The previous volumes which have been published in this series have contained versions belonging to what we may call the conscious period of romantic literature; the writers had not only a story to tell, but had also a very distinct feeling for the literary form of that story and the characterisation of the actors in it. In this present volume we go behind the work of these masters of their craft to that great mass of floating popular tradition from which the Arthurian epic gradually shaped itself, and of which fragments remain to throw here and there an unexpected light on certain features of the story, and to tantalise us with hints of all that has been lost past recovery.

All who have any real knowledge of the Arthurian cycle are well aware that the Breton lais, representing as they do the popular tradition and folk-lore of the people among whom they were current, are of value as affording indications of the original form and meaning of much of the completed legend, but of how much or how little value has not yet been exactly determined. An earlier generation of scholars regarded them as of great, perhaps too great, importance. They were inclined indiscriminately to regard the Arthurian romances as being but a series of connected lais. A later school practically ignores them, and sees in the Arthurian romances the conscious production of literary invention, dealing with materials gathered from all sources, and remodelled by the genius of a Northern French poet.

I believe, myself, that the eventual result of criticism will be to establish a position midway between these two points, and to show that though certain of the early Celticists exaggerated somewhat, they were, in the main, correct—their theory did not account for all the varied problems of the Arthurian story, but it was not for that to be lightly dismissed. The true note of the Arthurian legend is evolution not invention; the roots of that goodly growth spring alike from history, myth, and faëry; whether the two latter were not, so far as the distinctively Celtic elements of the legend are concerned, originally one, is a question which need not here be debated.[1]

This much is quite certain; while the mythic element in the Arthurian story is yet a matter for discussion, while we are as yet undecided whether Arthur was, or was not, identical with the Mercurius Artusius of the Gauls; whether he was, or was not, a Culture Hero; whether Gawain does, or does not, represent the same hero as Cuchullin, and both alike find origin in a solar myth; we at least know that both Arthur and Gawain are closely connected with, and as their final destination found rest in, Fairyland. It is, therefore, no matter for surprise if we

---

[1] In this connection, cf. Mr. Nutt's "Fairy Mythology of Shakespeare"—Popular Studies, No. 6.

find such definitely fairy stories as the lais of Guingamor and Lanval (which, be it noted, represent a whole family of kindred tales) connected with the Arthurian cycle, and their heroes figuring as knights of Arthur's court.[2]

At that court the fairy, whether she be Morgain, the Lady of the Lake, or the Mistress of Graalent, Lanval, or Gawain, is at home, to be distinguished by nothing, save her superior beauty and wisdom, from the mortals who surround her. (It is scarcely necessary to remark that the fairies of the mediæval French romance writers are not the pigmies of the Teutonic sagas and of Shakespeare.) The rôle of these maidens is, generally speaking, a clearly defined one: they are immortals in search of a mortal love,[3] and in this character the parallels carry us far back to the earliest stages of Celtic tradition as preserved in ancient Irish romance.

A special feature of these Breton lais, to be noted in this connection, is that they often combine two features which are more generally found apart, and which, as represented by their most famous mediæval forms, are wont to be considered by us as belonging to two different families of tradition, i.e., the Tannhäuser legend (the carrying off of a knight by the queen of the other world),

---

[2] Cf. Dr. Schofield's studies of the lais of Guingamor, Graalent, and Lanval, referred to in the Notes.
[3] To this rule Nimue, = the Lady of the Lake, appears to be the only exception.

and the Lohengrin legend (the rupture of a union between a mortal and an immortal, and the penalties incurred by the former by the transgression of a prohibition imposed by the latter). Two of the stories given in this volume, Guingamor and Lanval, in common with others which will be found noted in Dr. Schofield's studies, combine both motifs.

Now that such tales as these, in themselves independent popular folk-tales, sometimes became incorporated with, at other times by the loan of incident and feature strongly influenced, the Arthurian story, cannot I think be denied. Fairies such as the mistresses of Guingamor and Lanval were, as I have said above, residents or visitors at Arthur's court. Arthur himself is, like those knights, carried to Avalon; even as Guingamor in the extremity of mortal weakness. That like Guingamor he was thought of as recovering, and reigning with undiminished vigour over his fairy kingdom, is clear from numerous references in mediæval romance. The authors of La Bataille de Loquifer and Ogier le Danois knew him as King of Avalon; in Huon de Bordeaux he has been promised the reversion of Oberon's kingdom; in Lohengrin he reigns with Parzival, in a mysterious other-world realm; he is as completely lord of Fairyland as any knight beloved of fairy queen. The boyhood of Tyolet is the boyhood of Perceval; the mysterious stag guarded by lions wanders in and out of the mazes of Arthurian romance.

4

Some might, of course, suggest that these stories are really fragmentary borrowings from the Arthurian legend; but such a view is scarcely compatible with the fact that in their earlier forms they are entirely unconnected with that story. Thus we see that the lai of Guingamor in the solitary version we possess knows nothing of Arthur; neither the king or the queen, the fairy or her kingdom is named; Chrétien de Troyes knew the lady as Morgain, and her land as Avalon, and brings Guingamor to Arthur's court. The same remark applies to Graalent, while Lanval is in an Arthurian setting. If the stories had originally formed part of the cycle it is difficult to see why they should have been separated from it; while we can well understand that already existing folk-tales would be swept into the vortex of an increasingly popular tradition.

The story of Tyolet as preserved in the lai is certainly not in its earliest form; it is in some points incomprehensible, and as I have suggested in the Notes, the real meaning of the tale has been already forgotten. But Tyolet is never elsewhere mentioned as one of Arthur's knights, and the adventure achieved by him when transferred to Lancelot loses even the measure of coherence and plausibility it had preserved. Thus Lancelot, though knowing what is to be the guerdon of the successful knight, and voluntarily undertaking the adventure, when achieved, leaves the lady under the pretext of summoning his kinsmen and never returns; on no account would he be faithless to Guinevere.

5

In the Were-Wolf, again, the characters are anonymous; but Malory's reference leaves no room for doubt that the hero later on figured as one of Arthur's knights.

It is, I think, impossible to avoid the conclusion that the Arthurian legend, in the process of evolution, borrowed with both hands from already existing stores of popular folk-lore and tradition; and an examination of the parallels with this folk-lore element makes it equally clear that it was largely of Celtic origin.

But in what form was this popular tradition when the literary masterpieces of the Arthurian cycle, the poems of Chrétien de Troyes and his German rivals, were composed? We know that many of these tales were told as Breton lais, and in this original form they have practically disappeared. Those we possess are French translations, and of these the best and largest collection we owe to the skill and industry of Marie de France, an Anglo-Norman poetess who lived in the reign of Henry II. and was therefore a contemporary of Chrétien de Troyes. Of the four lais here given, two, Lanval and Were-Wolf (Bisclaveret), are undoubtedly by her, and Guingamor is very generally considered to be also her work. The metre in which she wrote was the eight-syllable verse, in rhymed pairs, adopted also by Chrétien in common with most of the poets of his time. As we see, Marie, like Chrétien, connected some of these lais with Arthur. They are Breton lais; Arthur is a Breton king; his legend certainly came to the Northern French poets partly, if not entirely, from Breton sources; the probability, therefore, is that the connection took place, in the first instance, on Breton rather than on French ground—i.e., it is due neither to Marie nor to Chrétien, but to the sources they used.

Setting hypothesis aside, however, this may be stated as an absolute matter of fact: at the time that the longer Arthurian romances took shape there were also current a number of short poems, both in Breton and in French, the latter in the precise metre adopted for the longer poems, connecting the Arthurian story with a great mass of floating popular folk-tale, which short poems were known to the writers of the longer and more elaborate romances. Are we seriously called upon to believe that they made absolutely no use of them? That they left all this wealth of material rigidly on one side, and combined for themselves out of their inventive faculties and classical knowledge the romances that won such deserved repute? Such a solution of the Arthurian problem I can scarcely think likely in the long run to be accepted by serious students; certainly not by those whom the study of comparative religion and folk-lore has taught how widely diffused in extension, and how persistent in character, are the tales which belong to the childhood of the race. That a large and important body of genuine existing tradition should be, not merely superseded, but practically beaten out of the field and destroyed by the power of mere literary invention, would be a curious phenomenon at any date; in the twelfth century it is absolutely inconceivable. The Arthurian legend has its roots in folk-tradition, and the abiding charm of its literary presentment is in reality due to the persistent vitality and pervasive quality of that folk-lore element. Children of a land of eternal youth, Arthur and his knights are ever young; it is true that some of the romances tell us that in the last great war with Lancelot Arthur was over ninety years old and Gawain above seventy, but one feels that even for the writer such figures had no significance; their words and actions are the words and actions of youth—we have here no Charlemagne and his veterans à la barbe fleurie.

But this is an element which in our rightful appreciation of the literary masterpieces of the cycle we are apt to ignore, nor is it other than scantily represented in English literature; it has therefore been thought well, in such a series as this to include a volume which shall direct attention less to the completed Arthurian epic than to the materials from which that epic was formed, since if we mistake not, it is to the nature of that material even more than to the skill of its fashioners, that the unexampled popularity of the Arthurian legend is due.

Bournemouth, May 1900

Guingamor

"Graislemiers de Fine Posterne
I amena conpeignons vint,
Et Guigomars ses frere i vint;
De l'Isle d'Avalon fu sire.
De cestui avons oi dire
Qu'il fu amis Morgain la fee,
Et ce fu veritez, provee."

Chretien de Troyes.—Erec. vv. 1952-58.

I will tell ye here a fair adventure, nor think ye that 'tis
but mine own invention, for 'tis truth, this tale I tell ye,

and men call the lay wherein 'tis writ the lay of Guingamor.

In Brittany of old time there reigned a king who held all the land in his sway, and was lord of many noble barons—his name I cannot tell ye. This king had a nephew who was both wise and courteous, a very brave and skilful knight, and Guingamor was he called. For his bravery and his beauty the king held him passing dear, and thought to make him his heir since he had no son. All men loved Guingamor; he knew how to promise, and how to give; knights and squires alike honoured him for his frankness and his courtesy; and his praises went abroad throughout all that land.

One day the king went forth to hunt and to disport himself in the forest. His nephew had that morn been bled and was still feeble, so might not go forth into the woodland, but would abide in his hostel, and with him were many of the king's companions.

At prime Guingamor arose and went forth to the castle to seek solace. The seneschal met him and threw his arm around his neck, and they spake together awhile, and then sat them down to play at chess. And as they sat there the queen came even to the door of the chamber, on her way to the chapel. She was tall and fair and graceful; and there she stood awhile to gaze on the knight whom she saw playing chess, and stayed her still and moved not.

Very fair did he seem to her in form and face and feature; he sat over against a window, and a ray of sunlight fell upon his face and illumined it with a fair colour. And the queen looked upon him till her thoughts were changed within her, and she was seized with love for him, for his beauty and his courtesy.

Then the queen turned her back, and called a maiden, and said: "Go thou to the knight who sitteth within playing chess, Guingamor, the king's nephew, and bid him come to me straightway."

So the maiden went her way to the knight, and bare him her lady's greeting, and her prayer that he come forthwith and speak with her; and Guingamor let his game be, and went with the maiden.

The queen greeted him courteously, and bade him sit beside her; but little did he think wherefore she made such fair semblance to him.

The queen spake first: "Guingamor, thou art very valiant, brave and courteous and winning—a fair adventure awaits thee—thou canst set thy love in high places! Thou hast a fair and courteous friend, I know neither dame nor damsel in the kingdom her equal! She loveth thee dearly, and thou canst have her for thy love."

The knight answered: "Lady, I know not how I can dearly love one whom I have never seen nor known; never have I heard speak of this aforetime, nor have I besought love from any."

And the queen spake: "Friend, be not so shamefaced; me canst thou very well love, for of a sooth I am not to be refused; I love thee well and will love thee all my days."

Then Guingamor was much abashed, and answered discreetly: "Well do I know, lady, that I ought to love thee; thou art wife to my lord the king, and I am bound to honour thee as my liege lady."

But the queen answered: "I say not that thou shalt love me thus, but I would love thee as my lover, and be thy lady. Thou art fair, and I am gracious; if it be thy will to love me very joyful shall we both be," and she drew him towards her and kissed him.

Guingamor understood well what she said, and what love she desired of him, and thereof had he great shame, and blushed rosy-red, and sprang up thinking to go forth from the chamber. The queen would fain keep him with her, and laid hold on his mantle, so that the clasp broke and he came forth without it.

12

Then Guingamor went back to the chessboard, and seated himself, much troubled at heart; so startled had he been that he had no thought for his mantle, but turned to his game without it.

The queen was much terrified when she thought of the king, for when Guingamor had so spoken, and showed her his mind she feared lest he should accuse her to his uncle. Then she called a maiden whom she trusted much, and gave her the mantle, and bade her bear it to the knight; and she laid it around his shoulders, but so troubled in mind was he that he knew not when she brought it to him; and the maiden returned to the queen.

So were the two in great fear till vesper-tide, when the king returned from the chase and sat him down to meat. They had had good sport that day, and he and his comrades were very joyful. After meat they laughed and made sport, and told their adventures, each spake of his deeds, who had missed, who had hit fair. Guingamor had not been with them, whereof he was sorrowful. So he held his peace, and spake no word.

But the queen watched him, and thinking to make him wrathful, she devised words of which each one should weigh heavily. She turned herself to the knights and spake: "Much do I hear ye boast, and tell of your adventures, yet of all whom I see here is none brave enough (were one to give him a thousand pounds of gold) to dare hunt or wind horn in the forest here without, where the white boar wanders. Marvellous praise would he win who should take that boar!"

Then all the knights held their peace, for none would assay that venture. Guingamor knew well that it was for him she spake thus. Throughout the hall all were silent, there was nor sound nor strife.

The king answered her first: "Lady, thou hast often heard of the adventure of the forest, and this thou knowest; it displeaseth me much when in any place I hear it spoken of. No man may go thither to hunt the boar who may return therefrom, so adventurous is the land, and so perilous the river. Much mischief have I already suffered; ten knights, the best of the land, have I lost; they set forth to seek the boar and came never again."

Then he said no more, but the company departed from each other, the knights went to their hostel to slumber and the king betook himself to his couch.

Guingamor did not forget the word which he had heard, but went his way to the king's chamber and knelt before him. "Sire," he said, "I ask of thee somewhat whereof I have great need, and which I pray thee to grant me, nor in any wise to refuse the gift."

The king said: "Fair nephew, I grant thee what thou

14

prayest from me, ask securely, for in naught would I deny thy will."

The knight thanked him, and said: "This is that which I demanded, and the gift which thou hast given me. I go to hunt in the forest." Then he prayed him to lend him his horse, his bloodhound, his brachet, and his pack of hounds.

When the king heard what his nephew said, and knew the gift he had given, he was very sorrowful and knew not what to do. Fain would he have taken back his word and bade him let the matter be, for such a gift should he not have asked; never would he suffer him, even for his weight in gold, to go chase the white boar, for never might he return. And if he lent him his good brachet and his steed then would he lose them both and never see them again, and naught had he that he valued so highly; there was nothing on earth he would have taken for them—"an I lose them I shall grieve all the days of my life."

And Guingamor answered the king: "Sire, by the faith I owe thee, for naught that thou could'st give me, were it the wide world, would I do other than I have said and chase the boar to-morrow. If thou wilt not lend me thy steed, and the brachet thou dost hold dear, thy hound and thine other dogs, then must I e'en take my own, such as they are."

With that came the queen who had heard what Guingamor desired (and know ye that it pleased her well), and she prayed the king that he would do as the knight required, for she thought thus to be delivered from him, and never, in all her life, to see him again. So earnestly did she make her prayer that at length the king granted all she might ask. Then Guingamor prayed leave, and went joyful to his dwelling; naught might he sleep that night, but when he saw dawn he arose in haste and made ready, and called to him all his companions, the king's household, who were in much fear for him, and would gladly have hindered his going an they might. He bade them bring him the king's steed which he had lent him the night before, and his brachet, and his good horn, which he would not have given for its weight in gold. Two packs of the king's good dogs did Guingamor take with him, and forgat not the bloodhound. The king himself would accompany him forth from the town, and with him came the burghers and the courtiers, rich and poor, making great cry and lamentation, and with them too were many ladies sorrowing sorely.

To the thicket nearest the city went all the huntsmen, taking with them the bloodhound, and seeking for the track of the wild boar, for they knew well where he was wont to haunt. They found the track and knew it, for many a time had they seen it, and traced the beast to his lair in the thick bushes and loosed the bloodhound, and by force drove forth the boar.

16

Then Guingamor sounded his horn and bade them uncouple one pack of dogs and the other lead forward to await him near the forest, but they should not enter therein. Thus Guingamor began the chase and the boar fled before him, leaving his lair unwillingly. The dogs followed, giving tongue, and hunted him to the verge of the forest, but further might they not go, since they were weary, wherefore they uncoupled the others. Guingamor rode on winding his horn, and the pack ran yelping on the boar's track; return to his lair he might not, but plunged into the forest, and the knight followed after, carrying the brachet which he had borrowed from the king.

They who had borne him company, the king and his fellowship and the men of the city, stayed without the wood, nor would go further. There they abode so long as they might hear the blast of the horn and the barking of the dogs, and then they commended the knight to God and turned them back to the town.

The boar ran further and further till he had wearied out the dogs, then Guingamor took the brachet and loosened the leash, and set it on the track, which it followed of right good will, while the knight did what he might to aid and encourage his uncle's dog by blowing gaily on his horn. Much did the sounds of the chase please him, but ere long he had lost both brachet and boar, he heard neither yelp nor cry and became sorrowful and much

17

displeased; he deemed he had lost the brachet through the thickness of the forest, and he was passing sorrowful for the sake of his uncle who loved the dog so well. So he went still forward into the forest, and coming to a high hill he stayed awhile, very sorrowful and much at a loss.

The sky was clear and the day fair, all around him sang the birds but he hearkened not to their song. Ere long he heard the brachet give tongue afar off and he began to wind his horn, troubled at heart till he saw the dog. Through a little plantation towards the open ground he saw the brachet and the boar come swiftly, and thought to reach them easily. He spurred his steed to a gallop, nor would delay, rejoicing much at heart and saying to himself that might he take the boar, and return whole and unharmed to court, he would win much fame, and his deed would be spoken of for all time.

In the joy of his heart he set the horn to his lips and blew a marvellous great blast. Afore him passed the boar with the brachet close upon its track. Guingamor rode after swiftly, through the adventurous land, across the perilous river, over the meadowland where the turf was green and flowery; well nigh had he overtaken his prey when he looked ahead and saw the walls of a great palace, well built, yet without mortar. 'Twas all enclosed of green marble, and above the entry was a tower which seemed to him of silver, so great was the clearness it gave. The doors were of fine ivory, inlaid with golden trefoils, nor was there bar nor lock.

Guingamor came on swiftly, and when he saw the door stand wide and the entrance free, he thought him he would go within and find the goodman who kept the gate, for fain would he know who was lord of the palace, since 'twas the fairest he had ever seen. Much it pleased him to look upon its beauties, for he thought he might lightly overtake the boar ere it had run far, since it was wearied by the chase. So he rode within and drew bridle in the palace, and looked all around, but no man might he see, naught was there about him but fine gold; and the chambers which opened from the hall seemed of stones of Paradise. That he found neither man nor woman there pleased him not, else was he glad that he had found so fair an adventure to tell again in his own land.

Then he turned him back, and rode quickly through the meadows by the river, but naught did he see of his boar, quarry and dog were alike lost. Then was Guingamor wrathful. "Of a truth," he said, "I am betrayed, men may well hold me for a fool. Methinks that to look upon a house have I lost all my labour. If I find not my dog and my boar little joy or pleasure shall I have henceforward, and never more may I return to my own land." Much troubled, he betook himself to the high ground of the forest, and began to listen if he might hear the cry of the dog.

Then he heard the brachet give tongue afar off to his right hand, and he waited and hearkened till he surely heard both dog and boar. Then he began again to wind his horn, and rode towards them. The boar passed before him, and Guingamor rode after, encouraging the brachet with hue and cry.

Thus he came into the open country, and found a spring beneath an olive tree, wide-spreading, and covered with leaves. The water of the spring was clear and fair, and the gravel thereof gold and silver. In the water a maiden was bathing herself while another combed her hair and washed her feet and hands. Fair was she, long-limbed and softly rounded, in all the world was there nothing so fair, neither lily nor rose, as that naked maiden.

As soon as Guingamor beheld her he was stirred by her beauty. He saw her garments on a bush, and turned his horse's bridle thither; he stayed not, but taking her robes, set them high in the fork of a great oak. When he had taken the boar, he thought to return and speak with the maiden, for he knew well that she would not go thence naked. But the maiden saw his deed, and called the knight to her, and spake proudly: "Guingamor, let be my robes; an God will, never shall it be told among knights that thou didst so discourteous a deed as to hide the garments of a maiden in the fork of a tree! Come hither, and fear not. To-day shalt thou abide with me, thou hast laboured all day and hast had but ill success."

Then Guingamor went towards her, and proffered her robe, and thanked her for her courtesy, and said he might not lodge with her, since he must seek the boar and the brachet which he had lost.

The maiden answered him: "Friend, all the knights in the world let them labour as they might should not find those two, an I gave them not mine aid. Let that folly be, and make this covenant with me; come with me and I pledge thee loyally that I will give thee the boar as a prize, and the brachet shalt thou have again to take with thee into thine own land, on the third day hence."

"Fair lady," said the knight, "by this covenant will I gladly abide even as thou hast spoken."

Then he dismounted, and the maiden clad herself in a short space, and she who was with her brought her a mule well and richly harnessed, and a palfrey, better had never count nor king. Guingamor lifted the maiden to her saddle, and rode beside her, holding her bridle in his hand. Often did he look upon her, and seeing her so fair and tall and graceful of good will would he become her lover. He looked upon her gently, and prayed her earnestly that she would grant him her love; never aforetime had his heart been troubled for any woman he had looked upon, nor had he thought of love.

The maiden, who was wise and courteous, answered

Guingamor that she would willingly grant him her love, whereof the knight was joyful, and since she had pledged herself to be his lady, he laid his arm around her and kissed her.

The waiting maiden had ridden on quickly to the palace wherein Guingamor had entered, and they had decked it richly, and bidden the knights mount and ride out to meet their lady, to do honour to the lover whom she brought with her. Three hundred or more of them there were, nor was there one but was clad in vest of silk wrought with gold thread. Each knight led with him his lady. 'Twas a passing fair company. There were squires with hawks, and fair falcons that had passed their moulting. In the palace were there as many playing at chess and other games.

When Guingamor dismounted he beheld the ten knights who had gone forth to chase the boar, and been lost from his land. They rose from their seats to meet him, and greeted him right joyfully, and Guingamor kissed them each one. A fair lodging was his that night, great plenty of rich meats, with much rejoicing, and great state; there was the sound of harps and viols, the song of youths and maidens. Much did he marvel at the noble fare, the beauty and the richness of all around. He bethought him that he would abide there two days, and on the third would take his way homeward; the dog and the boar would he take, and make known to his uncle the adventure which had befallen him, then would he return again to his lady.

Yet otherwise than he deemed had it chanced to him; not three days but three hundred years had he been in that palace; dead was the king, and dead his household and the men of his lineage, and the cities he had known had fallen into destruction and ruin.

On the third day Guingamor prayed leave of his love that he might go to his own land, and that she would give him the brachet and the boar, according to her covenant; and the maiden answered: "Friend, thou shalt have them, but know that thou wilt go hence for naught; 'tis three hundred years past since thou camest hither, thine uncle and his folk are dead; neither friends nor kinsmen shalt thou find. One thing I tell thee, ask where thou wilt, nowhere shalt thou find a man so old that he may tell thee aught of those thou seekest."

"Lady," quoth Guingamor, "I may not believe that thou sayest sooth, but if the thing be so then I swear to thee that I will straightway return hither."

And she answered, "I charge thee when thou hast passed the river to return to thine own land, that thou neither eat nor drink, however great may be thy need, till thou return once more to this land, otherwise art thou undone."

Then she bade them bring his steed, and the great boar, and the brachet which she gave him in leash, and Guingamor took the boar's head, more might he not carry, and mounted his steed and went forth. His lady rode with him to the river, and had him put across in a boat, then she commended him to God and left him.

The knight rode forward and wandered till midday in the forest, nor might he find a way out. 'Twas all so ill-looking and overgrown that he might know the way no longer. Then afar to the left he heard the axe of a wood-cutter, who had made a fire and burnt charcoal, and he spurred towards the sound, and gave the man greeting, and asked where his uncle the king abode, and at what castle he should seek for him.

But the charcoal-burner answered: "Of a faith, sire, I know naught; the king of whom thou speakest 'tis over three hundred years since he died, he and all his folk, and the castles of which thou askest have long been in ruins. There are certain of the old folk who full oft tell tales of that king, and of his nephew who was a wondrous valiant knight, how he went one day to hunt within this forest and was seen no more." Guingamor heard what he said, and a great pity seized him for the king his uncle, whom he had thus lost, and he spake to the charcoal-burner: "Hearken what I say to thee, for I will tell thee what has befallen me. I am he who went hunting in this forest, and I thought to return and bring with me the white boar." Then he began to tell of the palace he had found, and the maiden whom he had met, how she had lodged him royally for two days; "and on the third did I depart, and she gave me my dog and the boar." Then he gave him the boar's head and bade him keep it well till he returned to his home, and might tell the folk of the land how he had seen and spoken with Guingamor the king's nephew.

The poor man thanked him, and Guingamor bade him farewell, and turned him back and left him. 'Twas already past nones and the day drew towards vesper-tide; so great a hunger seized the knight that he became well-nigh ravening; by the roadside as he went there grew a wild apple tree, the boughs well laden with fruit; he drew near and plucked three and ate them. He did ill in that he forgat his lady's command, for even as he tasted the fruit he was aged and undone, so feeble of limb that he fell from his steed, and might move neither hand nor foot; when he might speak he began in a feeble voice to bemoan himself.

The charcoal-burner had followed him and seen what had chanced, and it seemed to him that he might scarce live till the evening. But as he would go to his aid there came riding two fair maidens, well and richly dressed, who dismounted beside Guingamor, and blamed him much, and reproached him for that he had so ill kept his lady's command. Gently they lifted the knight and set

25

him on his horse, and led him to the river, where they placed him, his steed, and his dog, in a boat and rowed them over.

The peasant turned him back, and that night he sought his home bearing with him the boar's head; far and wide he told the tale, and affirmed it by his oath. The head he gave unto the king, who caused it to be shown at many a feast; and that none might forget the adventure the king bade make a lay which bare the name of Guingamor— and so do the Breton call it.

Sir Launfal

This is the adventure of the rich and noble knight Sir Launfal, even as the Breton lay recounts it.

The valiant and courteous King, Arthur, was sojourning at Carduel, because of the Picts and the Scots who had greatly destroyed the land, for they were in the kingdom of Logres and often wrought mischief therein.

In Carduel, at Pentecost, the King held his summer court, and gave rich gifts to the counts, the barons, and all the knights of the Round Table. Never before in all the world were such gifts given. Honours and lands he shared forth to all, save to one alone, of those who served him.

This was Sir Launfal; of him and his the King thought not; and yet all men loved him, for worthy he was, free of hand, very valiant, and fair to look upon. Had any ill happened to this knight, his fellows would have been but ill-pleased.

Launfal was son to a king of high descent, but his heritage was far hence in a distant land; he was of the household of King Arthur, but all his money was spent, for the King gave him nothing, and nothing would Launfal ask from him. But now Sir Launfal was much perplexed, very sorrowful, and heavy of heart. Nor need ye wonder at it, for one who is a stranger and without counsel is but sorrowful in a foreign land when he knows not where to seek for aid.

This knight of whom I tell ye, who had served the King so well, one day mounted his horse and rode forth for diversion. He left the city behind him, and came all alone into a fair meadow through which ran a swift water. As he rode downwards to the stream, his horse shivered beneath him. Then the knight dismounted, and loosening the girth let the steed go free to feed at its will on the grass of the meadow. Then folding his mantle beneath his head he laid himself down; but his thoughts were troubled by his ill fortune, and as he lay on the grass he knew nothing that might pleasure him.

Suddenly, as he looked downward towards the bank of

the river, he saw two maidens coming towards him; never before had he seen maidens so fair. They were richly clad in robes of purple grey, and their faces were wondrous beautiful. The elder bore in her hands a basin of gold finely wrought (indeed it is but truth I tell you); the other held a snow-white towel.

They came straight to where the knight was lying, and Launfal, who was well taught in courteous ways, sprang to his feet in their presence. Then they saluted him, and delivered to him their message. "Sir Launfal," said the elder, "my lady, who is most fair and courteous, has sent us to you, for she wills that you shall return with us. See, her pavilion is near at hand, we will lead you thither in all safety."

Then Launfal went with them, taking no thought for his steed, which was grazing beside him in the meadow. The maidens led him to the tent, rich it was and well placed. Not even the Queen Semiramis in the days of her greatest wealth and power and wisdom, nor the Emperor Octavian, could have equalled from their treasures the drapery alone.

Above the tent was an eagle of gold, its worth I know not how to tell you; neither can I tell that of the silken cords and shining lances which upheld the tent; there is no king under heaven who could purchase its equal, let him offer what he would for it.

Within this pavilion was a maiden, of beauty surpassing even that of the lily and the new-blown rose, when they flower in the fair summer-tide. She lay upon a rich couch, the covering of which was worth the price of a castle, her fair and gracious body clothed only in a simple vest. Her costly mantle of white ermine, covered with purple of Alexandria, had she cast from her for the heat, and face and throat and neck were whiter than flower of the thorn. Then the maiden called the knight to her, and he came near and seated himself beside the couch.

"Launfal," she said, "fair friend, for you have I come forth from my own land; even from Lains have I come to seek you. If you be of very truth valiant and courteous then neither emperor, count nor king have known such joy as shall be yours, for I love you above all things."

Then Love smote him swiftly, and seized and kindled his heart, and he answered:

"Fair lady, if it so please you, and such joy may be my portion that you deign to love me, then be the thing folly or wisdom you can command nothing that I will not do to the utmost of my power. All your wishes will I fulfil, for you I will renounce my folk and my land, nor will I ever ask to leave you, if that be what you most desire of me."

When the maiden heard him whom she could love

30

well speak thus she granted him all her heart and her love.

And now was Launfal in the way to good fortune. A gift the lady bestowed upon him: there should be nothing so costly but that it might be his if he so willed it. Let him give or spend as freely as he would he should always have enough for his need. Happy indeed was Launfal, for the more largely he spent the more gold and silver should he have.

"Friend," said the maiden, "of one thing must I now warn you, nay more, I command and pray you, reveal this your adventure to no man. The reason will I tell you; if this our love be known you would lose me for ever, never again might you look upon me, never again embrace me."

Then he answered that he would keep faithfully all that she should command him.

Thus were the two together even till the vesper-tide, and if his lady would have consented fain would Launfal have remained longer.

"Friend," said she, "rise up, no longer may you linger here, you must go and I must remain. But one thing will I tell you, when you wish to speak with me (and I would that may ever be when a knight may meet his lady without shame and without reproach) I shall be ever there at your will, but no man save you shall see me, or hear me speak."

When the knight heard that he was joyful, and he kissed his lady and rose up, and the maidens who had led him to the tent brought him new and rich garments, and when he was clad in them there was no fairer knight under heaven. Then they brought him water for his hands, and a towel whereon to dry them, and laid food before him, and he supped with his lady. Courteously were they served, and great was the joy of Sir Launfal, for ever and again his love kissed him and he embraced her tenderly.

When they were risen from supper his horse was brought to him, saddled and bridled; right well had they tended it. Then the knight took leave of his lady, and mounted and rode towards the city; but often he looked behind him, for he marvelled greatly at all that had befallen him, and he rode ever thinking of his adventure, amazed and half-doubting, for he scarcely knew what the end thereof should be.

Then he entered his hostel and found all his men well clad, and he held great state but knew not whence the money came to him. In all the city there was no knight that had need of lodging but Launfal made him come unto him and gave him rich service. Launfal gave costly, gifts; Launfal ransomed prisoners; Launfal clothed the minstrels; Launfal lavished wealth and honours; there was neither friend nor stranger to whom he gave not gifts. Great were his joy and gladness, for whether by day or by night he might full often look upon his lady, and all things were at his commandment.

Now in the self-same year, after the feast of St. John, thirty of the knights went forth to disport themselves in a meadow, below the tower wherein the queen had her lodging. With them went Sir Gawain and his cousin, the gallant Iwein. Then said Gawain, the fair and courteous, who was loved of all: "Pardieu, my lords, we do ill in that we have not brought with us our companion, Sir Launfal, who is so free-handed and courteous, and son to so rich a king." Then they turned back to his hostelry, and by their prayers persuaded Launfal to come with them.

It so chanced that the queen leant forth from an open casement, and three of her chosen ladies with her. She looked upon Sir Launfal and knew him. Then she called one of her ladies, and bade her command the fairest and most graceful of her maidens to make ready and come forth with her to the meadow. Thirty or more she took with her, and descended the stairway of the tower. The knights were joyful at their coming, and hastened to meet them, and took them by the hand with all courtesy. But Sir Launfal went apart from the others, for the time seemed long to him ere he could see his lady, kiss her, and hold her in his arms. All other joys were but small to him if he had not that one delight of his heart.

When the queen saw him alone she went straight towards him, and seated herself beside him; then, calling him by his name, she opened her heart to him.

"Launfal," she said, "greatly have I honoured, cherished and loved you. All my love is yours if you will have it, and if I thus grant you my favour, then ought you to be joyful indeed."

"Lady," said the knight, "let me be; I have small desire of your love. Long have I served King Arthur; I will not now deny my faith. Neither for you nor for your love will I betray my liege lord."

The queen was angry, and in her wrath she spoke scoffingly. "They but spake the truth," she said, "who told me that you knew not how to love. Coward and traitor, false knight, my lord has done ill to suffer you so long about him; he loses much by it, to my thinking."

When Sir Launfal heard that he was wroth, and answered her swiftly, and by misfortune he said that of which he afterwards repented sorely. "Lady," he said, "you have been ill-advised. I love and I am loved by one who deserves the prize of beauty above all whom I know. One thing I will tell you, hear and mark it well;

one of her serving maidens, even the meanest among them, is worth more than you, my lady queen, in face and figure, in beauty, wisdom, and goodness."

Then the queen rose up and went weeping to her chamber, shamed and angered that Launfal should have thus insulted her. She laid herself down on her bed as if sick; never, she said, would she arise off it till the king did justice on the plaint she would lay before him.

King Arthur came back from the woods after a fair day's hunting and sought the queen's chamber. When she saw him she cried out, and fell at his feet, beseeching his favour, and saying that Sir Launfal had shamed her, for he had asked her love, and when she refused him had mocked and insulted her, for he had boasted of his lady that she was so fair, so noble, and so proud that even the lowest of her waiting women was worth more than the queen.

At this King Arthur fell into a rage, and swore a solemn oath that unless the knight could defend himself well and fully in open court, he should be hanged or burnt.

Forth from the chamber went the king, and called three of his barons to him, and bade them fetch Sir Launfal, who indeed was now sad and sorry enough. He had returned to his hostelry, but alas! he learnt all too soon that he had lost his lady, since he had revealed the secret of their love. He was all alone in his chamber, full of anguish. Again and again he called upon his love, but it availed him nothing. He wept and sighed, and once and again fell on the ground in his despair. A hundred times he besought her to have mercy on him, and to speak once more to her true knight. He cursed his heart and his mouth that had betrayed him; 'twas a marvel he did not slay himself. But neither cries nor blows nor lamentations sufficed to awaken her pity, and make her show herself to his eyes.

Alas, what comfort might there be for the unhappy knight who had thus made an enemy of his king? The barons came and bade him follow them to court without delay, for the queen had accused him, and the king, by their mouth, commanded his presence. Launfal followed them, sorrowing greatly; had they slain him it would have pleased him well. He stood before the king, mute and speechless, his countenance changed for sorrow.

The king spoke in anger: "Vassal," he said, "you have greatly wronged me; an evil excuse have you found to shame and injure me, and insult the queen. Foolish was your boast, and foolish must be your lady to hold that her maid-servant is fairer than my queen."

Sir Launfal denied that he had dishonoured himself or insulted his liege lord. Word by word he repeated what the queen had said to him; but of the words he himself had spoken, and the boast he had made concerning his love, he owned the truth; sorrowful enough he was, since by so doing he had lost her. And for this speech he would make amends, as the court might require.

The king was sorely enraged against him, and conjured his knights to say what might rightfully be done in such a case, and how Launfal should be punished. And the knights did as he bade them, and some spake fair, and some spake ill. Then they all took counsel together and decreed that judgment should be given on a fixed day; and that Sir Launfal should give pledges to his lord that he would return to his hostelry and await the verdict. Otherwise, he should be held a prisoner till the day came. The barons returned to the king, and told him what they had agreed upon; and King Arthur demanded pledges, but Launfal was alone, a stranger in a strange land, without friend or kindred.

Then Sir Gawain came near, with all his companions, and said to the king: "Take pledges of all ye hold of mine and these my friends, fiefs or lands, each for himself." And when they had thus given pledges for him who had nothing of his own, he was free to go to his hostelry. The knights bore Sir Launfal company, chiding him as they went for his grief, and cursing the mad love that had brought him to this pass. Every day they visited him that they might see if he ate and drank, for they feared much that he would go mad for sorrow.

At the day they had named the barons were all assembled, the king was there, and the queen, and the sureties delivered up Launfal. Very sorrowful they were for him. I think there were even three hundred of them who had done all in their power without being able to deliver him from peril. Of a great offence did they accuse him, and the king demanded that sentence should be given according to the accusation and the defence.

Then the barons went forth to consider their judgment, heavy at heart, many of them, for the gallant stranger who was in such stress among them. Others, indeed, were ready to sacrifice Launfal to the will of their seigneur.

Then spoke the Duke of Cornwall, for the right was his, whoever might weep or rage, to him it pertained to have the first word, and he said:

"The king lays his plea against a vassal, Launfal ye call him, of felony and misdeed he accuses him in the matter of a love of which he boasted himself, thus making my lady, the queen, wrathful. None, save the king, has aught against him; therefore do ye as I say, for he who would speak the truth must have respect unto no man, save only such honour as shall be due to his liege lord. Let Launfal be put upon his oath (the king will surely have naught against it) and if he can prove his words, and bring forward his lady, and that which he said and which so angered the queen be true, then he shall be pardoned; 'twas no villainy that he spake. But if he cannot bring proof of his word, then shall we make him to know that the king no longer desires his service and gives him dismissal from his court."

Then they sent messengers to the knight, and spake, and made clear to him that he must bring forth his lady that his word might be proved, and he held guiltless. But he told them that was beyond his power, never through her might succour come to him. Then the messengers returned to the judges, who saw there was no chance of aid, for the king pressed them hard, urged thereto by the queen, who was weary of awaiting their judgment.

But as they arose to seek the king they saw two maidens come riding on white palfreys. Very fair they were to look upon, clad in green sendal over their white skin. The knights beheld them gladly, and Gawain, with three others, hastened to Sir Launfal and told him what had chanced, and bade him look upon the maidens; and they prayed him eagerly to say whether one of the twain were his lady, but he answered them nay.

The two, so fair to look upon, had gone forward to the palace, and dismounted before the daïs whereon King Arthur was seated. If their beauty was great, so also was their speech courteous.

"King," they said, "command that chambers be assigned to us, fair with silken hangings, wherein our mistress can fitly lodge, for with you will she sojourn awhile."

They said no more, and the king called two knights, and bade them lead the maidens to the upper chambers.

Then the king demanded from his barons their judgment and their verdict, and said he was greatly wroth with them for their long delay.

"Sire," they answered, "we were stayed by the coming of the damsels. Our decision is not yet made, we go but now to take counsel together." Then they reassembled, sad and thoughtful, and great was the clamour and strife among them.

While they were yet in perplexity, they saw, descending the street, two maidens of noble aspect, clad in robes broidered with gold, and mounted on Spanish mules. Then all the knights were very joyful, and said each to the other: "Surely now shall Sir Launfal, the valiant and courteous, be safe."

Gawain and six companions went to seek the knight. "Sir," they said, "be of good courage, for the love of G'od speak to us. Hither come two damsels, most beautiful, and richly clad, one of them must of a truth be your lady!" But Launfal answered simply; "Never

40

before to-day have I looked upon, or known, or loved them."

Meantime, the maidens had come to the palace and stood before the king. Many praised them for their beauty and bright colour, and some deemed them fairer even than the queen.

The elder was wise and courteous, and she delivered her message gracefully. "King," she said, "bid your folk give us chambers wherein we may lodge with our lady; she comes hither to speak with you."

Then the king commanded that they should be led to their companions who had come before them. Nor as yet was the judgment spoken. So when the maidens had left the hall, he commanded his barons to deliver their verdict, their judgment already tarried too long, and the queen waxed wrathful for their delay.

But even as they sought the king, through the city came riding a maiden, in all the world was none so fair. She rode a white palfrey, that bore her well and easily. Well shaped were its head and neck, no better trained steed was there in all the world. Costly were the trappings of that palfrey, under heaven was there no king rich enough to purchase the like, save that he sold or pledged his land.

41

And thus was the lady clad: her raiment was all of white, laced on either side. Slender was her shape, and her neck whiter than snow on the bough. Her eyes were blue, her skin fair. Straight was her nose, and lovely her mouth. Her eyebrows were brown, her forehead white, and her hair fair and curling. Her mantle was of purple, and the skirts were folded about her; on her hand she bare a hawk, and a hound followed behind her.

In all the Burg there was no one, small nor great, young nor old, but was eager to look upon her as she passed. She came riding swiftly, and her beauty was no mere empty boast, but all men who looked upon her held her for a marvel, and not one of those who beheld her but felt his heart verily kindled with love.

Then those who loved Sir Launfal went to him, and told him of the maiden who came, if by the will of heaven she might deliver him. "Sir knight and comrade, hither comes one, no nutbrown maid is she, but the fairest of all fair women in this world." And Launfal heard, and sighed, for well he knew her. He raised his head and the blood flew to his cheek as he made swift answer: "Of a faith," he said, "this is my lady! Now let them slay me if they will and she has no mercy on me. I am whole if I do but see her."

The maiden reached the palace; fairer was she than any who had entered there. She dismounted before the king that all might behold her; she had let her mantle fall that they might the better see her beauty. King Arthur, in his courtesy, had risen to meet her, and all around him sprang to their feet, and were eager to offer their service. When they had looked well upon her, and praised her beauty, she spoke in these words, for no will had she to delay:

"King Arthur, I have loved one of your knights, behold him there, seigneur, Sir Launfal. He hath been accused at your court, but it is not my will that harm shall befall him. Concerning that which he said, know that the queen was in the wrong; never on any day did he pray her for her love. Of the boast that he hath made, if he may by me be acquitted, then shall your barons speak him free, as they have rightfully engaged to do."

The king granted that so it might be, nor was there a single voice but declared that Launfal was guiltless of wrong, for their own eyes had acquitted him.

And the maiden departed; in vain did the king pray her to remain; and many there were who would fain have served her. Without the hall was there a great block of grey marble, from which the chief knights of the king's court were wont to mount their steeds; on this Launfal took his stand, and when the maiden rode forth from the palace he sprang swiftly upon the palfrey behind her. Thus, as the Bretons tell us, he departed with her for that most fair island, Avalon; thither the fairy maiden had carried her knight, and none hath heard man speak further of Sir Launfal. Nor know I more of his story.

Tyolet

This is the Lay of Tyolet

A foretime when King Arthur reigned over the country of Britain, which is now called England, there were, I think me, far fewer folk in the land than there are to-day. But Arthur, whose valour men highly praise, had in his company many brave and noble knights. Of a sooth there are even now knights of high fame and renown, yet are they not such manner of men as they were of old time.

For then the best and bravest knights were wont to wander through the land seeking adventures by day and by night, with never a squire for company, and it might well be that in the day's journey they found neither house nor tower, or again perchance they would find two or three such. Or by dusky night they might find fair adventures, the which they would tell again at court, even as they had befallen. And the clerks of the court would write them fairly on parchment in the Latin tongue, so that in days to come, men, an they would, might hearken to them.

And these tales were turned from Latin into Romance, and from them, as our ancestors tell us, did the Britons make many a lay.

And one lay they made will I tell ye, even as I myself heard the tale. 'Twas of a lad, fair and skilful, proud and brave and valiant. Tyolet was he called, and he knew strange wiles, for by whistling could he call the beasts of the woodland to him and trap them, even as many as he would. A fairy had taught him this skill, and never a beast that God had made but would come to him at his whistle. A lady had he for mother, who dwelt in the wide woodland where her lord had made his abode by day and by night, and the spot was passing lonely, for ten leagues round was there no other dwelling.

Now the knight, his father, had been dead fifteen years, and Tyolet had grown fair and tall, but never an armed knight had he seen in all his days, and but rarely other folk in that wide woodland where his mother dwelt.

Never had he gone forth into the world beyond, for his mother held him passing dear, but in the forest might he wander as it pleased him, and no other pastime had he ever known. When he whistled as the fay had taught him, and the beasts heard him, then they came to him swiftly and he slew what he would and bore them home to his mother, and on this they lived, they twain alone, for neither brother nor sister had he, and his mother was a noble and courteous lady of good and loyal life.

One day she called her son unto her and prayed him gently (for she loved him much) to go into the wood and slay her a stag; and the lad at her command went straightway into the forest and wandered the groves till noontide, but neither stag nor beast of any kind might he see. Then he was sorely vexed at heart and bethought him to turn again homewards, since nothing might he find in the woodland, when under a tree he saw a stag which was both great and fair, and at once he whistled to it.

The stag heard his whistle and looked towards him, but it came not at his call nor awaited his coming, but at a gentle pace issued forth from the wood, and Tyolet followed it till it came to a water and passed over. The stream was deep and swift-flowing, wide-reaching and perilous to pass, and the stag stood safe upon the further shore. Tyolet looked up and down, and saw a roebuck fat and well-grown coming towards him, then he stayed his steps and whistled, and as the deer came closer he put forth his hand and drew his knife and plunged it into its body, and so slew it straightway.

But even as he did so he looked across the river, and lo! the stag which had passed the water changed its shape and became a knight, fully armed as a knight should be, and mounted on a gallant warhorse. Thus he stood on the river bank, and the lad, who never in his life had seen the like, deemed it a great marvel and stood silent, gazing long upon him, and wondering what might be the meaning of this strange gear.

Then the knight spake to him across the water with gentle words, courteously asking his name, and who he was and what he sought. And Tyolet answered him: "Son am I to the widow lady who dwelleth in the great forest, and Tyolet do they call me who would name my name. Now tell me who thou art, and what may be thy name?"

Then he who stood on the bank of the river spake: "Knight do men call me."

"What manner of beast may Knight be," quoth Tyolet; "where doth it dwell and whence doth it come?"

"Of a faith that will I tell thee, truly and with no lie. 'Tis a beast that is greatly feared for it taketh and eateth other beasts. Oft-times doth it abide in the wood and oft-times in the open lands."

"Of a faith," said Tyolet, "'tis a marvel—for never since I might wander in the wilderness have I seen such a beast; yet know I bears and lions, and every sort of venison. Nor is there a beast in all the forest that I know not, but I take them all without pain or trouble; thou alone I may not know. Yet thou seemest a brave beast. Tell me, thou Knight-Beast, what dost thou bear on thy head? And what is it that hangeth at thy neck, and is red and shining?"

"Of a truth I will tell thee, and lie not. That which I bear on my head is a coif, which men call helmet, with steel all around; and this is a mantle in which I am wrapped, and this at my neck a shield, banded with gold."

"And with what hast thou clad thyself, it seemeth me pierced through with little holes?"

"'Tis a coat of wrought mail, men call it a hauberk."

"And with what art thou shod? Tell me of thy friendship."

"Shoes and greaves of iron have I, right well wrought."

"And what hast thou girt at thy side? Tell me an thou wilt."

"Men call it a sword, 'tis fair to look upon, and the blade is hard and keen."

"And that long wood thou holdest? Tell me, and hide it not from me."

"Dost wish to know?"

"Yea, of a truth."

"'Tis a lance, this that I bear with me. Now have I told thee the truth of all thou hast required of me."

"Sir," quoth Tyolet, "I thank thee, and I would to God that I had also such vesture as thou hast, so fair and so comely; a coat and a coif and mantle even as thou wearest. Tell me, Knight-Beast, for the love of God and His fair Feast, if there be other beasts such as thou and as fair to look upon?"

"Of a truth," spake the knight, "I will shew thee more than a hundred such."

For as the tale telleth in a little space there came through the meadow two hundred armed knights, all of the king's court; they had even taken a stronghold at his command,

and set it in fire and flames, and now they went their way homeward riding in three ranged squadrons.

The Knight-Beast spake to Tyolet and bade him come forward a little step and look beyond the river; and the lad did as he bade him, and saw the knights ride armed on their chargers; and cried aloud, "Now see the beasts who all bear coifs on their heads! Ne'er have I seen such a sight! If it please God and His fair Feast I too will be a Knight-Beast!"

Then the knight who stood on the bank of the river spake again and said: "Wilt thou be brave and valiant?"

"Yea, of a truth, I swear it to thee."

"Then go thy way, and when thy mother seeth thee, she will say, 'Fair son, tell me, what aileth thee, and of what art thou thinking?' and thou shalt answer that thou hast much to think on, for thou would'st fain be like a Knight-Beast which thou hast seen in the forest, and for that art thou thoughtful; and she will tell thee that it grieveth her much that thou hast seen such a beast which deceiveth and devoureth others. Then shalt thou say, Of a faith little joy shall she have of thee if thou may'st not be even such a beast, and wear such a coif on thy head; and when she heareth that, swiftly will she bring thee other raiment, coat and mantle, helm and sword, greaves, and a long lance, even as thou hast seen here."

Then Tyolet departed, for it seemed to him long ere he might be at home, and he gave his mother the roebuck he had brought, and told her all his adventures even as they had chanced. And his mother answered that it grieved her much that he had seen such a beast, "For it taketh and devoureth many another."

"Of a truth," said Tyolet, "now is it thus: if I may not be even such a beast as I saw, little joy shalt thou have of me henceforward." When his mother heard that she answered straightway that all the arms she had would she bring him, and she brought those which had belonged to her lord, and armed her son therewith, and when he was mounted on his horse he seemed indeed to be a Knight-Beast.

"Now," said she, "fair son, dost know what thou must do? Thou shalt go straight to King Arthur, and take good heed to my words, company not with man or woman save with those of gentle birth and breeding." Then she embraced and kissed him, and the lad went on his way, and journeyed for many days over hills and plains and valley, till he came to the court of King Arthur, that valiant and courteous monarch.

The King was seated at meat, for he was wont to be richly served, but Tyolet waited not at the hall entrance; clad even as he was in his armour and mounted on his steed, he rode up to the daïs, whereon sat Arthur the King, and spake no word, nor gave greeting to any man.

"Friend," quoth the King, "dismount, and come, eat with us. Then shalt thou tell me what thou seekest, and who thou art, and what men call thee."

"Of a truth," said the lad, "I will tell thee that ere ever I eat. King, my name is Knight-Beast; many a beast have I slain, and men call me Tyolet. Well do I know how to catch venison, for, an it please thee, sire, I am son to the widow of the forest, and of a surety she hath sent me to thee to learn skill and wisdom and courtesy. I would learn of knighthood, of tourney, and jousting, how I may spend, and how I may give, for never aforetime came I in a king's court, and I think me well that never again shall I come where I may learn such fair nurture and courtesy. Now have I told thee what I seek. What is thy mind thereon, Sir King?"

And Arthur said, "Sir Knight, thou shalt be my man, come now and eat."

"Sire," he said, "I thank thee well."

Then Tyolet dismounted, and they disarmed him and clothed him in a surcoat and light mantle, and brought water for his hands and he sat down to meat.

With that there entered a maiden, a proud and noble lady; of her beauty I may not speak, but I deem well that neither Dido nor Helen herself was so fair. She was daughter unto the King of Logres, and came riding upon a snow-white palfrey, bearing with her a white brachet of smooth and shining hair, at whose neck hung a little golden bell. Thus she rode up before the King, and gave him greeting: "King Arthur, God the all powerful who reigneth on high have thee in His keeping."

"Fair friend, may He who counteth the faithful for His own guard thee."

"Sire, I am a maiden, daughter unto king and queen, and my father ruleth over Logres. I ask of thee for love, as of a right valiant monarch, if there be one among thy knights who is of such prowess that for me he will smite off the white foot of a certain stag. If there be give him to me, I pray thee, sire, and I will take him for my lord; for indeed, none other will I have. For no man may win my favour if he bring me not the white foot of that great and fair stag, the hair of which shineth like gold, and which is guarded by seven lions."

"Of a faith," said the King, "such covenant will I make with thee that he who bringeth hither the stag's foot shall have thee for wife."

"And I, Sir King, swear to thee that such shall be the covenant."

54

So they made the pact fast between them, and never a knight in the hall who was of any praise or renown but said he would go and seek the stag, did he but know where it might be found.

The maiden spake: "This brachet shall guide ye where the stag is wont to have his dwelling-place."

Then Lodoer, who desired greatly to be the first to seek the stag, prayed the boon from Arthur, and the King would not say him nay. So he took the brachet, and mounted and set forth to seek the stag's foot. But the dog which went with him led him straight to a water which was great and wide, black, swollen, and hideous to look upon, four hundred fathoms was it wide, and well on a hundred deep, and the brachet sprang straightway into the flood, deeming perchance, as a dog may, that the knight was following it closely.

But follow it would Lodoer in no wise: he had no mind to enter the stream, for he had little desire of death, and he said within himself: "He who hath not himself hath naught; he keepeth a castle well, I think me, who taketh heed that it be not mishandled."

Then the dog came forth out of the water, and returned to Lodoer, and Lodoer turned himself again and took the brachet, and went swiftly on his way to the court, where was a great company assembled, and gave back her brachet to the maiden, the King's daughter of Logres.

Then King Arthur asked him if he had brought the foot; and Lodoer answered that an another would risk his life, the venture yet awaited him. Then they mocked at him throughout the hall, but he wagged his head at them and bade them go seek the foot, if by hap they might bring it back.

Then many set forth to seek the stag, and to win the damsel, but never a one might sing another song than that which Lodoer of need must sing (for he was indeed a valiant knight) save one only, who was brave and swift-footed, and whom men called Knight-Beast, though his name, as ye know well, was Tyolet. For this knight went his way to King Arthur, and prayed him straitly that the maiden be held at the court for him, since he would go forth to conquer the adventure of the stag's foot; never, he said, would he return till he had smitten off the white right foot of the stag.

The King gave him leave, and Tyolet armed himself right well, and went to the maiden and prayed of her the loan of her white brachet, which she granted him freely, and he took leave of her. When he had ridden and roved long enough he came to the ford of that great and rushing water which was deep and deadly to look upon; the brachet sprang into the stream, and swam straightway, and Tyolet plunged in after it and thus mounted on his steed he followed the dog till he came forth on dry land. And the brachet ran ever before him and guided him till he came to where he might see the stag; seven lions they were that guarded it, and loved it with a great love.

Then Tyolet looked, and saw the stag where it fed alone in a meadow, and none of the lions were near at hand; and he set spurs to his horse, and passed before it whistling as he went. The stag came swiftly towards him, and when Tyolet had whistled seven times it stood still. Then Tyolet drew his sword, and taking the white right foot in his hand smote it off at the joint, and hid it within his robe. The stag at this gave a loud cry, and the lions, who were none too far off, came swiftly to its aid and beheld the knight.

One of the lions sprang upon the steed Tyolet bestrode, and wounded it so sorely that it tore away all the skin and flesh from the right shoulder, and when Tyolet saw it he smote the lion a mighty blow in the chest, cleaving asunder nerve and sinew—and with that lion had he no more ado. The steed fell to the ground, and even as the knight sprang clear the lions were upon him on all sides. They tore the good hauberk from his back, and the flesh from his arms and ribs, and wounded him so sorely that they went nigh to devour him altogether. Sorely was he torn, but at last he slew them, though scarce might he be delivered from their claws. Then he fell senseless beside the lions, for so torn and mauled was he that he might not stand upright.

Now as he lay senseless there came thither a knight mounted upon an iron-grey steed, and drew his bridle, and looked upon the young knight, and lamented over him. Then Tyolet opened his eyes, and told him all that had chanced, and bade him take the foot from out his breast. This the knight did, rejoicing greatly within himself, for much had he longed to win that foot.

But as he turned his bridle to ride away, he bethought him that by chance the young knight might even yet live, and if he did, then ill would it be for him; so he turned himself back thinking to slay the knight there and then lest he challenge him later. So he drew his sword, and thrust Tyolet through the body, and went his way, thinking that he had slain him.

Then came that traitor knight to the court of King Arthur, and shewed the white foot, and demanded the hand of the maiden. But the white brachet, which had led Tyolet to the stag had he not brought—of that knew he naught.

Then he claimed by covenant that fair maiden, since, he said, he had smitten off the white foot of the stag and brought it to court. But the King, who was wise enow, demanded eight days' grace to await Tyolet's return, ere he would assemble his court, for he had with him but those of his household—good knights all, frank and courteous. So the knight must needs grant that respite— and abide at court till the eight days were ended.

But he knew not that that good and courteous knight, Sir Gawain, had set forth secretly to seek Tyolet, for the brachet had come back to court alone, and Gawain deemed surely it would guide him to the knight. And indeed it led him truly to the meadow where he found Tyolet lying lifeless among the lions.

When Gawain saw the knight and the slaughter he had wrought, he mourned the ill-chance greatly, and dismounting spake softly to his friend, and Tyolet answered him feebly, telling him what had brought him to this pass; and as he spake there rode up a maiden, fair to look upon, mounted upon a mule, and greeted Gawain courteously. Then Gawain returned her greeting, and called her to him, and embraced her, praying her very gently and very courteously that she would bear this knight, who was indeed a right valiant knight, to the leech of the Black Mountain; and the maiden did even as he besought her, and bare Tyolet to the leech, praying him to care for him for the sake of Sir Gawain.

The leech willingly received the knight, and did off his armour, laying him on a table. Then he washed his wounds, and freed them from the clotted blood which was all around them, and saw that he would do well, and

59

would be whole again within the month. But Sir Gawain went his way back to court and dismounted within the hall. And he found there the knight who had brought the white foot; he had dwelt at court till the eight days were passed, and now he came to the King, saluting him, and praying him to keep the covenant which the maiden of Logres had herself devised, and to which King Arthur had given consent—to wit, that whosoever should bring her the white foot, him would she take for lord; and King Arthur said, "'Tis the truth."

But when Gawain heard this he sprang forward swiftly, and said to the King: "Sire, 'tis not so; were it not that here before thee who art the king I may not give the lie to any man, be he knight or squire, I would say that he doth lie, and never won the white foot or the stag in the manner of which he vaunteth himself. Great shame doth he do to knights who would boast himself of another's deeds and clothe himself with another's mantle; who would steal the goods from another's store, and deck himself with that which belongeth to another; who by the hand of another would joust, and draw forth from the thicket the fearsome serpent. Nor shall it thus be seen in this court; what thou sayest is worth naught, make thine assault elsewhere, seek elsewhere for what thou desirest, this maiden is not for thee!"

"Of a faith," quoth the knight, "Sir Gawain, now dost thou hold me for a coward and a villain, since thou sayest that

I dare not lay lance in rest for jousting, and know how to steal goods from another's store, and draw the serpent from the thicket by another's hand. But thou speakest falsely as thou wilt find, if thou thinkest to prove thy words by force of arms, and deemest that thou wilt not find me in the field!"

While they thus strove together behold Tyolet, who had come thither in haste and had dismounted without the hall. The King rose from his seat to meet him, and threw his arms around his neck, and kissed him for the great love which he bare to him; and Tyolet bowed before him as fitting before his lord.

Then Gawain embraced him, and Urian, and Kay, and Yvain the son of Morgain, and the good knight Lodoer, and all the other knights.

But the knight who would fain win the maiden through the foot which Tyolet had given to him, and which he had brought thither, spake again to Arthur, and again made request.

But Tyolet, when he knew that he demanded the maiden, spake courteously to him, and asked him gently: "Sir Knight, tell me here in the presence of the King, by what right dost thou claim this maiden?"

"Of a faith," he said, "I will tell thee. It is because I

brought her the white foot of the stag; the King and she herself had so pledged it."

"Didst thou then smite off the foot? If it be true, it may not be denied."

"Yea, I smote it off, and brought it hither with me."

"And who then slew the seven lions?"

The knight looked upon him and said never a word, but reddened, and waxed wrathful.

Then Tyolet spake again: "Sir Knight, who was he who was smitten with the sword, and who was he who smote him? Tell me, I pray thee, for of a truth I think me that last wast thou!" And the knight frowned, as one ashamed.

"But that was, methinks, to return evil for good when thou didst that deed. In all good faith I gave thee the foot which I had smitten from off the stag, and for that didst thou give me such guerdon as went nigh to slay me; dead ought I to be in very truth. I gave thee a gift: of that do I now repent me. With the sword thou didst carry didst thou smite me through the body, thinking to have slain me. If thou would'st deny it, here will I tend to King Arthur my gage that I will prove it before this noble company."

But when the knight heard that, since he feared death more than shame, he cried him mercy, knowing that he spake truth. Nothing dared he gainsay, but yielded himself to King Arthur to do his commandment.

Then Tyolet, taking counsel with the King and his barons, pardoned him, and the knight fell on his knees and kissed his feet. Then Tyolet raised him up and kissed him, and from that day forward they spake no more of that matter. The knight gave back the stag's foot, and Tyolet gave it to the damsel.

The lily and the new-blown rose, when it bloometh first in the fair summer-time, are less fair than was that maiden. Then Tyolet prayed her hand in marriage, and with her consent did King Arthur give her to him. She led him back with her to her land, there was he king, and she queen—and here the lay of Tyolet findeth ending.

The Were-Wolf

"Sir Marrok, the good knight that was betrayed with his wife, for she made him seven year a Werwolf."—Morte D'Arthur, book xix. chap. 11.

In the days of King Arthur there lived in Brittany a valiant knight of noble birth and fair to look upon; in high favour with his lord and much loved by all his fellows. This knight was wedded to a fair and gracious lady whom he loved tenderly, and she too loved her lord, but one thing vexed her sorely—three days in every week would her husband leave her, and none knew whither he went, or what he did while thus absent.

And every time the lady vexed herself more and more, till at last she could no longer keep silence, and when her husband came back, joyful and glad at heart after one of these journeys, she said to him: "My dear lord, there is somewhat I would fain ask thee, and yet I scarce dare, for I fear lest thou be angry with me."

Then her lord drew her to him, and kissed her tenderly. "Lady," he said, "fear not to ask me, there is nothing I would not gladly tell thee, if it be in my power."

"I' faith," she said, "now is my heart at rest. My lord, didst thou but know how terrified I am in the days I am left alone; I rise in the morning affrighted, and lie down at night in such dread of losing thee that if I be not soon reassured I think me I shall die of it. Tell me, I pray thee, where thou goest, and on what errand, that I who love thee may be at rest during thine absence."

"Lady," he answered, "for the love of God ask me no more, for indeed if I told thee evil would surely come of it; thou would'st cease to love me, and I should be lost."

When the lady heard this she was but ill-pleased, nor would she let her lord be at peace, but day by day she besought him with prayers and caresses, till at length he yielded and told her all the truth. "Lady," he said, "there is a spell cast upon me: three days in the week am I forced to become a were-wolf; and when I feel the change coming upon me I hide me in the thickest part of the forest, and there I live on prey and roots till the time has expired."

When he had told her this his wife asked him what of his garments? Did he still wear them in his wolf's shape?

"Nay," he said, "I must needs lay them aside."

"And what dost thou do with them?"

"Ah, that I may not tell thee, for if I were to lose them, or they should be stolen from me, then must I needs be a wolf all my days, nothing could aid me save that the garments be brought to me again. So for my own safety I must needs keep the matter secret."

"Ah, my dear lord, why hide it from me? Surely thou hast no fear of me who love thee above all else in the world? Little love canst thou have for me! What have I done? What sin have I committed that thou should'st withdraw thy confidence? Thou wilt do well to tell me."

Thus she wept and entreated till at length the knight yielded, and told her all.

"Wife," he said, "without the forest on the highway, at a cross road, is an old chapel wherein I have often found help and succour. Close to it, under a thick shrub, is a large stone with a hollow beneath it; under that stone I hide my garments till the enchantment hath lost its power, and I may turn me homewards."

Now when the lady had heard this story it fell out even as her husband had foretold, for her love was changed to loathing, and she was seized with a great dread and fear of him. She was terrified to be in his presence, yet he was her lord, and she knew not how she might escape from him.

Then she bethought her of a certain knight of that country, who had loved her long, and wooed her in vain ere she wedded her lord; and one time when her husband went forth, she sent for him in secret, and bade him come and give her counsel on a matter that troubled her much. When he came she bade him swear an oath to keep secret what she might tell him, and when he had sworn she told him all the story, and prayed him for the sake of the love he once bore her to free her from one who was neither beast nor man, and yet was both.

The knight, who loved her still, was ready to do all she might desire, and she said, "'Tis but to steal his clothes, for then he can no more become a man, but must dwell in the forest as a wolf all his days, and some one will assuredly slay him." So he went forth, and did after her bidding and brought her the garments, and she hid them away saying, "Now am I safe, and that monster can return no more to terrify me."

When the time went on, and her husband came not, the lady feigned to be anxious for his welfare, and she sent his men forth to seek him; they went through all the country but could find no trace of their lord, so at length they gave up the search, and all deemed he had been slain on one of his mysterious journeys. And when a year had passed, and the lady thought the wolf had surely been killed, she wedded the knight who had aided her and thought no more of the husband she had betrayed.

But the poor were-wolf roamed the forest in suffering and sorrow, for though a beast outwardly yet he had the heart and brain of a man, and knew well what had happened, and he grieved bitterly, for he had loved his wife truly and well.

Now it chanced one day that the king of that land rode a-hunting in that very forest, and the hounds came on the track of the were-wolf and roused him from his lair and gave chase to him. All day he fled before them through the woodland, and at last when they were close upon him and he was in sore peril of being overtaken and torn in pieces the king came riding after the hounds, and the wolf swerved aside and fled to him, seizing him by the stirrup, and licking his foot in sign of submission.

The king was much astonished, and called to his companions to come swiftly. "See here, my lords," he said, "what think ye of this marvel? See how this beast entreats mercy of me; he hath the sense of a man! Drive off the dogs, for I will not have him injured. Turn we homewards, I take this beast in my peace, and will hunt no more in this forest lest by chance he be slain."

With that they turned their bridles and rode homewards; but the wolf followed behind, and would not be driven back, even when they came to the royal castle. The king was greatly pleased, for he thought the matter strange and marvellous; no such tale had he ever heard before; and since he had taken a great liking for the beast he bade his knights not merely to do the wolf no harm, but to treat him with all care and kindness, on pain of losing the royal favour. So all day the wolf roamed the court, free among the knights, and at night he slept in the king's own chamber. Wherever the king went, there he would have his wolf go too, and all the courtiers made much of the beast, seeing that it pleased their lord, and finding that he did no harm to any man among them.

Now when a long time had passed the king had occasion to hold a solemn court; he summoned all his barons from far and near, and among them came the knight who had betrayed the were-wolf, and wedded his lady; he had little thought that his rival was yet in life, still less that he was so near at hand. But as soon as the wolf beheld him he sprang upon him savagely, tearing him with his teeth, and would have slain him if the king had not called him off, and even then twice again he would have seized him.

Every one in the castle was astonished at the rage shown by the beast, which had always been so tame and gentle, and a whisper went round that surely there must be something which no one knew against the knight, for the wolf would scarce have attacked him without cause. All the time the court lasted the wolf had to be kept in close guard. When at length it broke up the knight who had been attacked was one of the first to leave—and small marvel it he were. But when the knight had gone the wolf was once more as tame and friendly as he had been from the first, and all the courtiers made a pet of him as they had done aforetime, and forgot, as time went on, that he had ever shown himself so savage.

At length the king bethought him that he would make a progress through his kingdom, and at the same time hunt for a while in the forest where he had found the wolf. As his custom was he took the beast with him.

Now the lady, the were-wolf's treacherous wife, hearing that the king would abide some time in that part of the country, prayed for an audience that she might win the royal favour by presenting rich gifts, for she knew well that the king loved not her second husband as he had loved the first.

The king appointed a day and hour for the audience, but when the lady entered the presence chamber suddenly the wolf flew upon her, and before any could hinder had bitten the nose from off her face. The courtiers drew out their weapons and would have slain the beast, when a wise man, one of the king's councillors, stayed them. "Sire," he said, "hearken to me—this wolf has been long with us, there is not one of us here who has not been near to him, and caressed him, over and over again; yet not a man of us has he ever touched, or even shown ill-will to any. But two has he ever attacked, this lady here and the lord, her husband. Now, sire, bethink thee well—this lady was the wife of the knight thou didst hold dear aforetime, and who was lost long since, no man knowing what came to him. Take my counsel, put this lady in guard, and question her closely as to whether she can give any reason why the wolf should hate her. Many a marvel hath come to pass in Brittany, and methinks there is something stranger than we wot of here."

The king thought the old lord's counsel good; he caused the lady and her husband to be put in prison apart, and questioned separately with threats if they kept silence; till at length the lady, terrified, confessed how she had betrayed her first husband, by causing his garments to be stolen from him when he was in a wolf's shape. Since that time he had disappeared; she knew not whether he were alive or dead, but she thought that perchance this wolf was he. When the king heard this he commanded them to fetch the garments belonging to the lost knight, whether it were pleasing to the lady or no; and when they were brought he laid them before the wolf and waited to see what would chance.

But the wolf made as if he saw them not, and the wise councillor said, "Sire, if this beast be indeed a were-wolf he will not change shapes while there are any to behold him; since it is only with great pain and difficulty he can do so. Bid them take wolf and garments into thine own chamber, and fasten the doors upon him; then leave him for a while, and we shall see if he become man."

The king thought this counsel good, and he himself took the beast into his chamber and made the doors fast.

Then they waited for a space that seemed long enough to the king, and when the old lord told him he might well do so, he took two nobles with him, and unlocked the doors, and entered, and lo, on the king's couch lay the long lost knight in a deep slumber!

The king ran to him and embraced him warmly; and when the first wonder had somewhat passed, he bade him take back all the lands of which he had been robbed, and over and above he bestowed upon him many rich gifts.

The treacherous wife and her second husband were

banished from the country; many years they lived in a strange land, and had children and grand-children—but all their descendants might be known by this, that the maidens were born without noses, so that they won the surname of énasées.

And the old books say that this adventure was verily true, and that it was in order that the memory of it should be preserved to all time that the Bretons put it in verse, and called it "The Lai of the Were-Wolf."

Notes

GUINGAMOR

This charming lay was first published by M. Gaston Paris (Romania VIII.) from the same MS. collection as the Lay of Tyolet. The author is unnamed, but the general consensus of critical opinion has attributed it to Marie de France, the famous Anglo-Norman poetess. Certainly both in manner and matter it is a remarkably favourable specimen of the Breton lay.

The story of Guingamor evidently represents a very favourite class of tales; setting aside the numerous parallels cited by Dr. Schofield in his study of the lay (The Lay of Guingamor, "Harvard Studies and Notes in Philology and Literature," vol. v.), we have among the French translations of Breton lays which have descended to us no fewer than three which closely correspond in subject and treatment, the lays of Guingamor, Graalent, and Lanval. In each of these the hero is tempted by a queen; rejects her proffered love; wins a fairy bride, and departs to dwell with her in her own land. Guingamor and Graalent agree in the circumstances under which the knight meets the fairy maiden (a feature in which Dr. Schofield sees the influence of the Wayland story—cf. The Lays of Graalent and Lanval, and the Story of

Wayland, W. H. Schofield); while Lanval and Graalent agree in the subsequent development of the story.

Of the three, Guingamor is distinctly the most tragic. The knight who after two days spent in the delights of love and the festivities of the wondrous palace returns on the third day to his own land to find that kinsmen and friends have passed away, and his own name and fate but a folk-tale centuries old, is a really pathetic figure. We need not wonder that the story was a popular one; not only does Chrétien de Troyes in the quotation prefixed to my translation mention it, but it is again referred to as a well-known tale by Gautier de Doulens, one of the continuators of Chrétien's unfinished Conte del Graal. The knight who is coupled with Guingamor in our extract, Graislemiers de Fine Posterne, is by Prof. Foerster and other scholars identified with Graalent mor, and it seems probable that it was the close resemblance between their stories, noted above, which led the French poet to represent them as brothers.

Page 6.—He knew how to promise and how to give. "Bien sot promestre et bien doner." This should be compared with Wace's description of Gawain, "plus volt faire que il ne dist, Et plus doner qu'il ne promist." It is impossible not to feel that Arthur's gallant nephew, who had a fairy for his love, and who according to Chaucer found his final home in fairy-land, stands in very close connection with these heroes of the earlier stratum of Arthurian legend.

Page 18.—Taking her robes set them high in the fork of a great oak. This apparently unknightly proceeding on the part of the hero was doubtless originally connected with the supernatural character of the lady, and seems to have taken its rise in a confusion between a fay and a swan-maiden. As we know from Northern tradition (Brynhild's Hell-reid and the Wieland-saga) to steal the "swan-shift" of such a maiden was the recognised means of effecting her capture. This has been well discussed by Dr. Schofield in the study quoted above.

I charge thee—that thou neither eat nor drink.

This is evidently a somewhat confused introduction of the well-known feature that partaking of food in any land brings the eater under the operation of the laws of that land, but we generally find the incident of reverse application, as in the case of Persephone, who having tasted of the pomegranate seeds must needs continue an inhabitant of the other world. Guingamor having already eaten of the food of faëry, would, one would think, be incapable of returning to the other world. Such a fate as befalls him is, however, often brought about by coming in contact with the earth; thus in the Voyage of Bran, when the hero and his companions return from the Magic Isles, they are warned not to set foot on the shore of Ireland; one of the company disobeys the injunction and immediately falls to ashes, as one many years dead. Mr. Hartland, in his work on The Science of Fairy-tales, gives other instances of this belief. From the references made to the story by later writers, however, it is quite clear that Guingamor was supposed to have regained his youth on his return to Fairyland, and to enjoy practical immortality as the lord of its queen.

SIR LAUNFAL

This is a translation of the Lai de Lanval, by Marie de France, the original source being, as in the case of all the other stories, a Breton lai which the Anglo-Norman poetess translated into French.

The English poem of the same name, by Thomas of Chester, is not, strictly speaking, a translation of Marie's lai, but an adaptation, into which features borrowed from other sources have been worked. Thus the author evidently knew the lay of Graalent, which, as I have stated in the note to Guingamor, recites precisely the same story as Lanval, only with certain variations in the incidents. Dr. Schofield, in the study to which I have previously referred, decides that the original hero is Lanval.

The Graalent version contains a weirdly pathetic feature

which was either unknown to Marie or disregarded by her. The hero rides off, not on the lady's steed, but on his own; crossing the river he is swept from the saddle, and only saved from drowning by his mistress, who takes him up behind her on her palfrey. The knight's charger, reaching the shore, vainly seeks for his master, and the Bretons tell how yearly, on the anniversary of Graalent's disappearance, the horse may be heard neighing loudly for the vanished knight. Thomas of Chester refers to this story evidently, but appears to think that the steed had rejoined its master, as after telling how "every yer, upon a certayn day, Men may here Launfale's stede nay," he goes on to tell how any who desires a joust to keep his arms from rusting "may fynde justes anow wyth Syr Launfal the knyght."

TYOLET

This lay is the translation of one published by M. Gaston Paris (Romania VIII. 1879) from a MS. in the Bibliothèque Nationale, and previously unknown. It will be seen that it really consists of two distinct stories: (a) Tyolet's Enfances; (b) his achieving of the adventure of the white-footed stag. Whether these two stories originally related to the same hero is doubtful, but both are of considerable importance for the criticism of the Arthurian legend.

(a) Tyolet's Enfances.—This story certainly bears a strong

78

resemblance to the "Perceval" story as related by Chrétien de Troyes and Wolfram von Eschenbach; but while in some points it seems to have preserved more archaic features, in others it is distinctly more modern. Thus the lad's confusion of the knight with a beast seems a primitive trait, as does also his fairy gift of attracting beasts by whistling, and the curious transformation of the stag, while his behaviour on arriving at court, on the other hand, is far more civilised than that of Perceval. One naturally asks where had he learnt of tourneys and joustings and the knightly duty of "largesse"? The probability is that we have here a revised, and independent, version of the popular folk-tale which under the hands of certain twelfth-century poets developed into the Perceval romance.

(b) Le cerf au pied blanc. This story is also found in the vast compilation of Arthurian romance known as the Dutch Lancelot. There the adventure is attributed to Lancelot, but with certain variants—e.g., Kay, and not Lodoer, is the first to attempt the adventure, and to fail through cowardice (a trait entirely in accord with the rôle played by Kay in the later Arthurian story); Lancelot slays the lions before cutting off the foot of the stag; and he does not marry the lady, who in this version has not herself visited Arthur's court but has sent a messenger. This at once points to a later redaction of the story; the hero certainly ought to marry the maiden at whose instigation he undertakes the adventure.

The part played by the traitor knight did not, I venture to think, originally belong to the story; it is part of a very widely spread Aryan folk-tale, generally relating to the slaying of a dragon or similar monster. Mr. Hartland has given a long list of the variants of this in The Legend of Perseus, vol. iii. A very fine specimen is contained in the early Tristan poems, notably that of Gottfried von Strassburg, and another version, that contained in the poem of Morien ascribes the adventure to Lancelot. It may be remarked that in both the "Lancelot" versions, as in this lai of Tyolet, it is Gawain who seeks the hero, and chivalrously defends his claim against that of the traitor. The story certainly must have become connected with the Arthurian legend at a time when Gawain was still the beau-ideal of knightly courtesy.

The original tale at the root of the Cerf au pied blanc was, I believe, a transformation tale; the stag was the enchanted relative of the lady who instigated the adventure, and the spell could only be broken by smiting off the animal's foot (as in many instances it is necessary to cut off the head of the victim of magic spells); this seems to me the only explanation of what is here a pointless act of cruelty. Probably the connecting link with the tale of Tyolet is the mysterious stag-knight of the first part, not the fairy gift of whistling as M. Gaston Paris suggested. I believe the story to be the origin of the white stag guarded by six lions in the Prose Lancelot, which in the "Queste" changes with its four attendant lions into

Our Lord and the Four Evangelists. The real meaning of the story has here been preserved. This solution is also indicated by the fact that one of the shapes assumed by Merlin in his numerous transformations is that of a stag with one white foot (cf. "Merlin," Sommer's edition, xxiii. p. 302).

In connection with this it may be noted that a story published in the Scottish Celtic Review, vol. i., "Macphie's Black Dog," contains a striking parallel to Tyolet. The hero goes forth to shoot and sees a royal stag, but whenever he raises his gun to fire the animal changes into a woman. I think it is clear that in Tyolet we have the Perceval Enfances plus a transformation tale.

THE WERE-WOLF

The source of this is the Lai du Bisclavaret, by Marie de France. She was evidently relating a popular tradition, and there can be little doubt that it is the story referred to by Malory in the passage quoted at the heading of the tale. In Marie's Lai none of the characters are named.

The same story appears to be at the root of a Celtic folk-tale, Morraha, published by Mr. Jacobs in his collection entitled, "More Celtic Fairy Tales," here, however, being only subsidiary, a story within a story. Elsewhere I have found no trace of it, but the reference in Malory appeared to justify its inclusion among Arthurian tales.

Since writing this note Mr. Nutt has drawn my attention to a tale published in the Scottish Celtic Review, referred to above, "How the Great Tuairisgeul was put to Death." This tale strongly resembles Morraha, only the transformation is brought about by the spells of a witch employed by the stepmother, and is not the deed of the wife. Morraha seems to occupy a position between our tale and this. It may be suggested that there is a certain resemblance between the name Morraha, and that given by Malory for the hero of the story Marrok. It is worth noting that in both these tales the sympathy of the reader is invited for the wolf. As a rule a were-wolf is an object of dread and abhorrence.

7526820R00051

Printed in Great Britain
by Amazon.co.uk, Ltd.,
Marston Gate.